Eighteen Woody Allen Films Analyzed

Also by Sander H. Lee

Woody Allen's Angst:
Philosophical Commentaries on His Serious Films
(McFarland, 1996)